Natural Parks of Texas

Sandra Colmenares

Translated by Christina Green

Rosen
YA
New York

Published in 2018by The Rosen Publishing Group
29 East 21st Street, New York NY 10010

Copyright © 2018 by The Rosen Publishing Group
All rights reserved. No part of this book may be reproduced
in any form without permission in writing from the publisher,
except by a reviewer.

LIBRARY OF CONGRESS CATALOGING-IN-PUBLICATION DATA

Names: Colmenares, Sandra.
Title: Natural Parks of Texas / Sandra Colmenares.
Description: New York : Rosen Publishing, 2018. |
Series: Explore Texas | Includes index.
Identifiers: ISBN 9781508186717 (pbk.) |
ISBN 9781508186632 (library bound)
Subjects: LCSH: Natural history–Texas–Juvenile literature. |
Texas–Juvenile literature.
Classification: LCC QH105.T4 C65 2018 | DDC 578.09764–dc23

Manufactured in the United States of America

PHOTO CREDITS
On the cover RIRF Stock/Shutterstock.com, p. 4 dibrova/Shutterstock.com (top), Blaine Harrington III/Corbis Documentary/Getty Images (bottom); p. 5 JB Manning/Shutterstock.com; p. 6 ericfoltz/E+/Getty Images (top), pr2is/Shutterstock.com (bottom); p. 7 Matthijs Nijkamp/Shutterstock.com (top), Brian Lasenby/Shutterstock.com (bottom); p. 8 Witold Skrypczak/Lonely Planet Images/Getty Images; p. 9 SLainez/Shutterstock.com (top), Joe Fara/Shutterstock.com (bottom); pp. 10–11 Brian S/Shutterstock.com; p. 10 Nativestock.com/Marilyn Angel Wynn/Nativestock/Getty Images (left), Matt Jeppson/Shutterstock.com (right); p. 11 image by WMay/Moment/Getty Images; p. 12 Mary E. McCabe/Shutterstock.com, Witold Skrypczak/Lonely Planet Images/Getty Images (bottom); p. 13 Stanley Ford/Shutterstock.com; pp. 14–15 Peter Wilson/Dorling Kindersley/Getty Images; p. 15 Dennis W Donohue/Shutterstock.com (top left), Cynthia Kidwell/Shutterstock.com (top right), mojoeks/Shutterstock.com (bottom); p. 16 Jupiterimages/Stockbyte/Getty Images; p. 16–17 Ivan Kuzmir/imageBROKER/Getty Images; p. 17 jimkruger/E+/Getty Image (top), Matt Hansen Photography. davemhuntphotography/Shutterstock.com (bottom); p. 18 Seth K. Hughes/Image Source/Getty Images; p. 19 Education Images/Universal Images Group (top), Danita Delimont/Gallo Images/Getty Images (middle), Dennis W Donohue/Shutterstock.com (bottom); p. 20 Fred LaBounty/Shutterstock.com; p. 21 Martha Marks/Shutterstock.com (top), Witold Skrypczak/Lonely Planet Images/Getty Images (middle), Danita Delimont/Gall Images/Getty Images (bottom); p. 22 Stephen Saks/Lonely Planet Images/Getty Images (top), George Grall/National Geographic/Getty Images (bottom).

Contents

Hamilton Pool is a natural preserve. It extends about 232 acres (94 hectares) with paths and trails to walk on.

Natural Preserves in Texas

Texas has around 100 parks and natural reserves within its borders. Some of them are areas dedicated to protecting the natural resources and **ecosystems** of Texas. This is one of the ways to **preserve** our **environment**.

Texan parks can be visited on foot, bicycle, or canoe in one day or more. You can also discover Texas's past by the archeological remains that exist in the parks. Around some of its main cities, including Houston, Austin, Dallas, San Antonio, and El Paso, there are natural protected areas that you can visit. Intrigued?

Hikers in Big Bend National Park. This park is in the Chihuahua Desert, the largest desert in North America.

Those Who Protect the Parks

Parks are public spaces. They are protected by government institutions as well as private organizations. In Texas, the Department of Parks and Wildlife and the National Park Service manage the parks.

The **park ranger** is the visitor's best friend. They care for and protect of the ecosystem of the park and, at the same time, they care that the visitors enjoy themselves. They maintain recreational areas, paths, and service installations.

The care of the park also depends a lot on the help of volunteers—people who love nature and want to help. Everyone works together to preserve and enjoy our parks!

Park ranger at the Padre Island National Park. One of their jobs is to register turtle spawning on the beach.

Bentsen-Rio Grande Valley

The Rio Grande starts in the central region of Colorado and flows to empty out in the Gulf of Mexico. Part of its route marks the border between the United States and Mexico.

Bird and Butterfly Paradise

The Bentsen-Rio Grande Valley Park is located in the southeast of Texas, along the shore of the Rio Grande. It is made up of a forest **bank** extending 795 ac. (309 ha).

The park **houses** more than 350 species of birds and more than 200 species of butterflies. There are also falcon observation towers. From these towers, you can see a part of Mexico.

During spring and fall each year, many groups of birds fly over the park. This is the time of the bird migration.

In summer, the broad-winged hawk (*Buteo platyptero*) lives along the coast of the United States, from Texas to Canada. In winter, they migrate to the Caribbean, Mexico, and to the south or Brazil.

The crystal butterfly gets its name from its transparent wings.

Vocabulary

aficionados people who practice an art or trade in a nonprofessional capacity.

bank margin or shore of a river or sea.

houses gives lodging or housing.

Crystal Butterfly

The lower region of the Rio Grande, in the south of Texas, is rich with a diversity of butterflies. Photography **aficionados** and enthusiasts of these species specially travel to this place to see them. There are about 300 species of butterflies living in this valley.

Many are rare species, like the crystal butterfly (*Greta morgane*). This butterfly has transparent wings with spots on its edges.

The crystal butterfly is very common in Mexico, Central America, and the Caribbean. However, since around 2003, they have also been seen flying around the Bentsen-Rio Grande Valley Park.

More Facts

Butterflies can be seen in the park throughout the whole year, but the best time to see a lot of them is from October to December, especially the rare species!

The golden fronted woodpecker lives in the south of Texas for most of the year. It is part of the red-bellied woodpecker family. Occasionally, these species cross over to reproduce.

QUICK FACT

In Mexico, the Rio Grande is called Rio Bravo and North Rio Bravo.

Caprock Canyons

Plateaus and Plains

The Caprock Canyons are located to the northwest of Texas, between New Mexico and Oklahoma.

The topography of the park is composed of **reddish** rock formations that measure up to 1,000 feet (300 meters) in height. There are also rivers, lakes, **fauna**, and vegetation.

The park has many paths to enjoy on foot, on bicycle, or on horseback.

There are long and short paths, for all preferences, from easy to the most difficult, that are available for mountain biking. There are around 90 miles (140 kilometers) of paths to walk on.

Very Interesting!

The Clarity Tunnel is part of the remnants of an old railway. Today, no trains pass through it. Among all that you can encounter, there are bats. Experts believe that, sometimes, there are up to half a million of them in the tunnel.

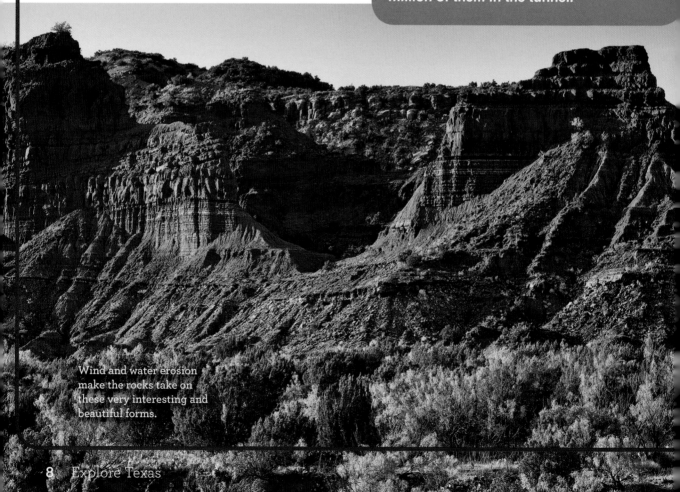

Wind and water erosion make the rocks take on these very interesting and beautiful forms.

Vocabulary

fauna group of animals in an area.

reddish red in color.

wander to walk without course, without a specific direction.

The bison herd has lived in the park since 1878. They represent one of the herds in the country formed to avoid complete extinction.

Bison Lands

Bison live freely in the Caprock Canyons park. They **wander** through the broad plains in a herd. However, there are not a lot of them. These bison are under the care and protection of the park, just like the other animals that they live with: coyotes, snakes, lynx, birds, lizards, deer, and other park dwellers. Many of the animals, especially the birds, drink water from Tao Lake. The eastern collared lizard is one of the fourteen species of lizards that run through the canyons and plains.

More Facts

The prairie dogs are the newest inhabitants of the park. They look very friendly but are very nervous. They live in a community, in interconnected tunnels that they construct under the ground.

The eastern collared lizard is just one of the many species of lizards that roam throughout the park.

Grand Canyon of Texas

The Grand Canyon of Texas is located to the South of the city of Amarillo, in Llano Estacado. It encompasses an area of approximately 118 mi. (190 km) long and 6 mi. (10 km) wide. Some places can be up to 980 ft. (300 m) deep.

The old Spanish colonists called it the Grand **Canyon** for its steep and abrupt landscape.

It is believed that it began forming 250 million years ago. Along the walls, you can see that each layer has a different color and represents a geological period.

Ancient Inhabitants of the Grand Canyon

The first inhabitants of the land were the Clovis and Folsom tribes.

The Clovis **culture** is considered the oldest and most extensive of the American continent.

It is possible to find **mortars** and ancient rock objects from these old cultures.

Very Interesting!

It is believed that the Folsom tribe built a city on Clovis lands in the park around 10,800 years ago. Archeological remains show that they were skilled large bison hunters and also ingenious builders of hunting tools.

Folsom

Clovis

The horned lizard of Texas is a protected species in the park. Its species is threatened by extinction.

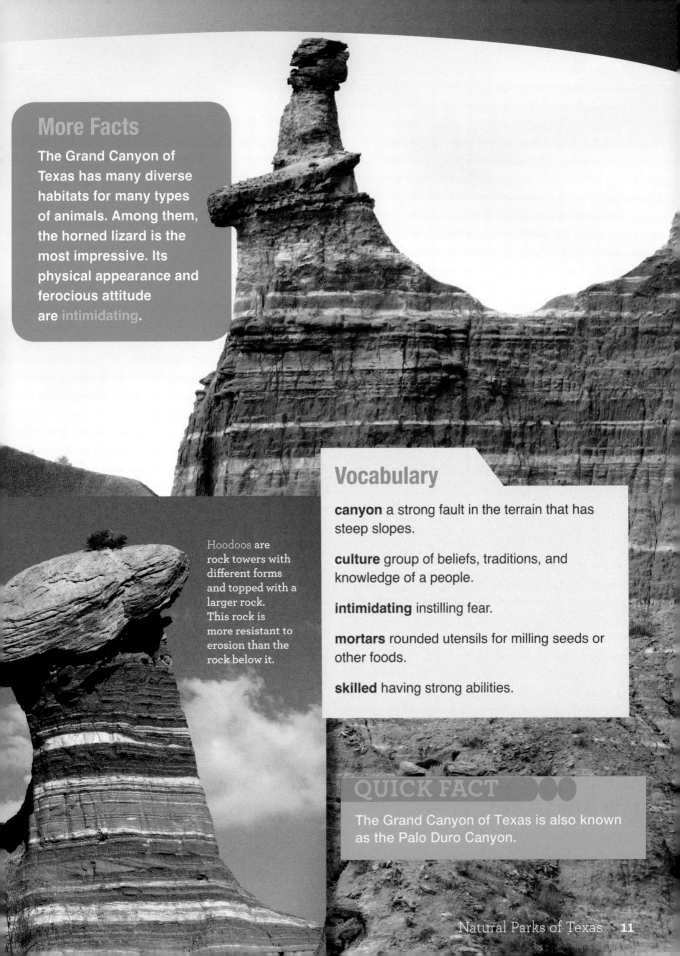

More Facts

The Grand Canyon of Texas has many diverse habitats for many types of animals. Among them, the horned lizard is the most impressive. Its physical appearance and ferocious attitude are intimidating.

Hoodoos **are** rock towers with different forms and topped with a larger rock. This rock is more resistant to erosion than the rock below it.

Vocabulary

canyon a strong fault in the terrain that has steep slopes.

culture group of beliefs, traditions, and knowledge of a people.

intimidating instilling fear.

mortars rounded utensils for milling seeds or other foods.

skilled having strong abilities.

QUICK FACT

The Grand Canyon of Texas is also known as the Palo Duro Canyon.

Pedernales and Gorman Falls

The broad limestone basin i
300 million years old. In its
wells, you can swim or just
enjoy the landscape.

Pedernales Falls

The Pedernales Falls State Park is near Austin. The Pedernales River traverses the park and forms waterfalls along the path. During the rainy season, the flow of the river can be very **turbulent**. Generally, however, there are calm waters for swimming and **splashing** around.

The river waters **snake** around limestone, irregularly distributed around the landscape. As a result, the current forms shallow and deep wells. The force of the water varies according to the surrounding area that molds it.

Another way to enjoy the lush nature of the park is to travel along the paths and trails, whether on foot or by bicycle. Additionally, it is a good place to camp comfortably, listening to the **murmur** of the running water.

Some areas have water falling some 164 ft. (50 m) for a dist
1.8 mi. (3 km). The best views are found to the north of the p

Gorman Falls

Not very far from the Pedernales Falls, in the heart of Texas, are the Gorman Falls. This area is like a small tropical forest.

It is found in Colorado Bend Park, west of the Colorado River, and close to the Gorman stream, which also supplies the falls. The big waterfall drops from a height of 60 ft. (18 m).

Around the base of the Colorado Bend canyons, there are hundreds of caves to explore.

Paths and trails surround the river, as well as campsites. Mountaineering enthusiasts enjoy scaling the mountains with the views of the river.

Waterfalls, paths, and caves to explore are some of the natural wonders of the Colorado Bend park.

Vocabulary

murmur noise, continuous sound.

snake to move or be shaped with bends.

splash to hit with water with your hands and feet; playing in the water.

turbulent when water is rushing and agitated.

QUICK FACT

Gorman Falls is one of the unique falls in Texas that has water throughout the year.

Village Creek

Cypress trees grow in the wetlands and serve as a refuge for birds and reptiles.

Village Creek Park is in the southeast part of Texas, in a natural reserve known as High Chaparral. Many types of ecosystems converge in the **dense** rainforests and flowing **streams**. Many species of animal and plant life prosper in them.

Some parts of the park extend over the marshes of the Neches River and Village Creek. If you go by canoe through its waters, it is possible to see beavers and river otters, as well as many types of fish, snakes, turtles, and toads. Along its banks, you may even discover some carnivorous plants!

The Lynx

Lynx are reddish or gray medium-sized wildcats. Its tail is short, but it has large, wide paws. It can live in any type of habitat. Its preferred areas are canyons and rocky areas. Lynx have a great ability to adapt and survive in more adverse natural conditions.

Vocabulary

adverse something contrary to what would be hoped; unfavorable.

dense very full; thick.

nocturnal characterized by being active at night.

streams short rivers.

The Opossum

The opossum is a species of weasel native to the area north of the Rio Grande. It is the size of a domestic cat. It leads a nocturnal and solitary life. It feed on plants, fruits, and animals such as rodents, birds, insects, crustaceans, or toads. Opossums in the wild typically only live short lives of two years.

The Otter

Otters are playful animals. They like to swim and slide on their stomachs over rocks into the water. However, they are shy animals and are rarely seen.

Powderhorn Ranch

The Powderhorn Ranch natural reserve covers 17,351 ac. (7 ha). Its landscapes consist of swamps with rich vegetation and abundant wildlife. This reserve is located on the coast of the Gulf of Mexico, near Matagorda Bay.

Among the oak forests, **estuaries**, prairies, and the sea live numerous migratory birds and other terrestrial and marine species. One of the great secrets that keeps wildlife alive here is the abundance of fresh water.

Powderhorn Ranch is not currently open to the public. It is a natural wildlife space. Park managers have opened a few areas for visitors. There, you can enjoy nature while canoeing, fishing, camping, swimming, and enjoy nature.

The roseate spoonbill is a type of heron. It gets its name from the coloring of its wings and the form of its beak.

The Whooping Crane

The whooping crane is a species of heron seen in Powderhorn, especially in the winter. This bird is at risk of extinction. However, it is thought that Powderhorn Ranch can help in the recovery of the species.

Vocabulary

brackish containing salt.

estuaries outlets of a river to the sea.

marsh land abundant in puddles and soft mud.

More Facts

In the spring, thousands of singing migratory birds find temporary refuge in Powderhorn to rest and feed.

Powderhorn Lake

It is a small and shallow lake. Its water is **brackish** and its soil is composed of sand, marine shells, and plants. The shore is composed of **marsh**. Among the fish that inhabit the lake are trout, red sea bass, and plaice. Some species of crocodile can be found in the wetlands.

Big Bend

Big Bend Ranch

Big Bend Ranch State Park is located in far western Texas. It **surrounds** the famous Chihuahua desert. The landscape of the park includes rivers, deserts, and mountains. Visitors can enjoy walks through desert areas of canyons and high **plateaus**. They can also navigate or walk around the Rio Grande, toward the southern **boundaries** of the park. Four of the largest events that mark the geological development of North America can be seen in this park. Scientists think the area was formed 35 million years ago.

The park offers unlimited opportunities to have fun and enjoy yourself.

iew of the Santa Elena Canyon and he Rio Grande in Big Bend Park.

ig Bend Park

ig Bend National Park is adjacent to Big Bend anch. Extending 800,000 ac. (323,748 ha), it ffers various opportunities for exploration and nvestigation. The black bear and the puma are ome of the treasures that the park protects.

he black bear is one of the largest mammals n North America. It eats plants and other nimals. One of its favorite plants is the sotol, a pecies of desert palm

he puma, or mountain lion, also lives in the ealm of the park. It is not very common, but ney like to **prowl** about the mountains and anyons, where they can hide. They feed on bbits, rodents, and ares, but their favorites re wild boar and deer.

A black bear with its cubs. It is rare to see them on paths.

The wild boar or wild hog mainly eats plants. It is also the lynx's favorite prey.

Very Interesting!

In the park caverns or on the rocks, you can walk in the footprints of the ancient inhabitants and explorers. There are animal, human, insect, and other figures painted here. Many of them are between 500 and 3,000 years old.

View of the Guadalupe and El Capitan peaks from the sandy plains of the Chihuahua desert.

Guadalupe Mountains

Coral Reefs

The Guadalupe Mountains are located in the northwest of Texas, by El Paso. They are surrounded by the Chihuahua desert. In the distant past, this chain of mountains was covered by the sea and marine life. Today, it constitutes the most impressive **fossil reef** in the world.

Guadalupe Peak

Guadalupe Peak is the highest point of the Guadalupe Mountains. It measures 9,800 ft. (3,000 m) in height. Some people call it the roof of Texas.

El Capitan

On the far southeast end of the Guadalupe Mountains is El Capitan peak. It is not as high as Guadalupe Peak, but many consider it to have an **imposing** presence.

Colors of Autumn on Guadalupe Peak

The shadow in the canyon and the permanent streams help life flourish in the desert. After October, the temperature drops and the colors reveal themselves in McKittrick Canyon.

The maple, oak, and ash trees dominate the autumn countryside. Their leaves **turn** shades of red and yellow.

i bloom in spring.
brilliant colors
eir flowers vary
een red
orange.

Vocabulary

fossil a trace of a living organism thas has been preserved.

imposing something extraordinary and impressive.

reef marine mountain composed of rock and corals.

turn to change from one way to another.

awn view of Guadalupe (*rear*) and El Capitán *ront*) peaks.

Very Interesting!

Some animals are nocturnal, and others are diurnal. During the day, species such as the wild boar, lizards, birds, mice, and rattlesnakes come out. At night, mountain cats, including the lynx and the puma, come out, as well as the raccoon, the ring-tailed cat, raccoon families, and bats.

The McKittrick Canyon paths are full of colors, from the changing of the tree leaves in the fall to the many different kinds of flowers in the area.

Padre Island

Malaquita Beach on Padre Island National Coastal Preserve.

The Padre Island National Coastal Preserve is composed of 62 mi. (100 km) of untouched coastline that separates the Gulf of Mexico from Laguna Madre. The park includes dunes, prairies, and shoreline beaches with a lot of marine life. It is also home to 380 species of birds, insects, amphibious reptiles, and butterflies.

Laguna Madre is one of six saltwater lagoons in the world. It has a higher salt concentration than the ocean.

The Kemp's ridley sea turtle comes to the Padre Island beach to spawn, lay eggs, and return to the sea. Once the hatchlings emerge, they quickly scurry toward the sea.

Very Interesting!

There have been three Spanish shipwrecks at the bottom of the Padre Island seas since 1554.

The Kemp's ridley sea turtle is at risk of extinction. Padre Island is an important refuge for it.

Glossary

adverse something contrary to what would be hoped; unfavorable.

aficionados people who practice an art or trade in a nonprofessional capacity.

bank margin or shore of a river or sea.

boundaries area limits; lines that separate some lands from others.

brackish containing salt.

canyon a strong fault in the terrain that has deep slopes.

culture group of beliefs, traditions, and knowledge of a people.

dense very full; thick.

ecosystems communities of living beings and their environment.

environment combination of external conditions that affect a living being.

estuaries outlets of a river to the sea.

fauna group of animals in an area.

fossil a trace of a living organism that has been preserved.

houses gives lodging or housing.

imposing something extraordinary and impressive.

intimidating instilling fear.

marsh land abundant in puddles and soft mud.

mortars rounded utensils for milling seeds or other foods.

murmur noise, continuous sound.

nocturnal characterized by being active at night.

park ranger someone in charge of caring for and maintaining parks.

plateaus high-rise plains.

preserve to protect and maintain something from any danger or damage.

prowl to wander or go free somewhere.

reddish red in color.

reef marine mountain composed of rock and corals.

skilled having strong abilities.

snake to move or be shaped with bends.

splash to hit with water with your hands and feet, playing in the water.

streams short rivers.

surrounds goes all the way around something.

turbulent when water is rushing and agitated.

turn to change from one way to another.

wander to walk without course, without a specific direction.

Index